D1449516

HIROSHIMA AND THE ATOMIC BOMB

by

Wallace B. Black
and
Jean F. Blashfield

CRESTWOOD HOUSE
New York

Maxwell Macmillan Canada
Toronto

Maxwell Macmillan International
New York Oxford Singapore Sydney

Library of Congress Cataloging-in-Publication Data

Black, Wallace B.
   Hiroshima and the atomic bomb / by Wallace B. Black and Jean F.
Blashfield. — 1st ed.
     p.   cm. — (World War II 50th anniversary series)
Includes bibliographical references.
   Summary: Describes the events surrounding President Truman's decision
to drop the atomic bomb on Hiroshima and Nagasaki, the devastating destruc-
tion of these cities, the Japanese surrender and the end of World War II.
   ISBN 0-89686-571-1
   1. Hiroshima – (Japan) – History – Bombardment, 1945 – Juvenile literature.
2. Atomic bomb – Juvenile literature. 3. World War, 1939-1945 – Campaigns –
Japan – Juvenile literature. I. Blashfield, Jean F. II. Title. III. Series: Black,
Wallace B. World War II 50th anniversary.
D767.25.H6B53 1993
940.54'25—dc20

92-33974

Created and produced by B & B Publishing, Inc.

Picture Credits
Dave Conant (map) - page 23
National Archives - pages 3, 4, 9, 10 (both), 12, 15, 17, 28, 34, 35, 36, 37, 40, 41, 43, 44, 45
United States Air Force - pages 19, 30, 39
United States Navy - page 25

**CRESTWOOD
HOUSE**

Macmillan Publishing Company
866 Third Avenue
New York, NY 10022

Maxwell Macmillan Canada, Inc.
1200 Eglinton Avenue East
Suite 200
Don Mills, Ontario M3C 3N1

Macmillan Publishing Company is part of the Maxwell Communication Group of Companies.

Printed in the United States of America

First Edition

10 9 8 7 6 5 4 3 2 1

CONTENTS

1. The Manhattan Project 5
2. Iwo Jima and Okinawa 13
3. Firebombing Japan 18
4. Invasion Plans..22
5. The Enola Gay 26
6. Hiroshima 31
7. Japan Surrenders 38
Glossary 46
Index 47

Chapter 1

THE MANHATTAN PROJECT

In 1939, when World War II began in Europe, conventional weapons were used by all armies and navies of the world. Tanks and artillery dominated ground warfare. Modern fighter and bomber aircraft made the air forces of the combatants take on new importance. Battles at sea were carried out by warships of conventional design both above and below the surface. Nuclear energy and the possibility of an atomic bomb were ideas beyond the comprehension of all except a few scientists in Europe.

Austrian scientist Lise Meitner, working with German scientists, was one of the first individuals to recognize the hidden power in the uranium atom. Following research conducted by Italian physicist Enrico Fermi, she studied neutron bombardment of uranium and as a result discovered the new element Uranium 235 (U^{235}). Although a native of Austria and a Jew, she was free from the German persecution of the Jews. However, when Hitler took over Austria, she was forced to flee to Sweden.

In 1939, working with her nephew, Otto Robert Frisch, Lise Meitner continued her studies of nuclear energy in Sweden. Based on the findings of two German physicists, she and Frisch published a paper suggesting that the nucleus of an atom of uranium, when bombarded by a

Allied prisoners of war in a Japanese prison camp cheer rescuers from the U.S. Navy. They are waving flags of the United States, Great Britain and the Netherlands.

single neutron, released three new neutrons. They in turn would strike other uranium atoms, causing a chain reaction.

Scientists predicted that this reaction would result in the release of tremendous amounts of energy. They had also determined that plutonium, a by-product of the production of U^{235}, the type of uranium that would later be used in an atomic bomb, could also be used to create an even more violent nuclear chain reaction.

Experimentation in the United States

Following the release of the Meitner and Frisch findings, scientists in the United States confirmed their theory. A small group of scientists at Columbia University in New York recognized the possibility of developing this new-found energy source as a military weapon. The Columbia scientists, some of whom had recently escaped from Germany, made efforts to interest the U.S. government in the research. They were worried that Germany might be successful in developing an atomic weapon first and thus be able to conquer the world.

World famous physicist Albert Einstein (right) *discussing plans for an atomic bomb with navy Captain Geoffrey E. Sage* (left) *and a fellow naval officer.*

The U.S. government, however, expressed no interest in supporting their research. Finally, in October 1939, the world-famous scientist Albert Einstein sent a personal letter to President Franklin D. Roosevelt, informing him of the military potential of newfound discoveries in atomic energy. As a result, the United States government began some modest additional research.

Nuclear physicists in the United States convinced the government that German scientists were also working on the development of atomic weapons and that U.S. research should be stepped up. In 1942, following the Japanese attack on Pearl Harbor, the United States made the final commitment to begin the development of the atomic bomb. In that year, a group of scientists including Dr. Enrico Fermi, working at the University of Chicago, created the first controlled chain reaction which would lead to the eventual production of atomic weapons.

The Manhattan Project

Responsibility for the development of an atomic bomb was given to a joint civilian and military organization headquartered in New York City. With offices in Manhattan, the project was given the name the "Manhattan Project." In September 1942, a U.S. Army officer, Leslie R. Groves, was put in charge of this nuclear research project.

Brigadier General Groves was a tough army career officer filled with unlimited energy and ambition. A strict disciplinarian, he was immediately disliked by the scientists who worked for him. At the same time, the general looked upon his widely scattered team of scientists with mistrust. It appeared that military discipline and scientific genius would not mix.

As a result, General Groves recognized the need for a civilian project director to work with him. He chose Dr. Julius Robert Oppenheimer, a young scientist from the University of California at Berkeley. It proved a perfect choice as Dr. Oppenheimer could communicate with his fellow scientists and was able to weave them into an effective working team.

Los Alamos, New Mexico

It soon became obvious that their team of scientists needed to work together at one location. General Groves and Dr. Oppenheimer started looking for a site for their top secret project. It needed to be hidden away from highly populated areas and still offer the necessary accommodations. A small boys' school near Los Alamos, New Mexico, was chosen. It was far from any major city and had ample space for the large staff that would be required. Located in high, rugged mountainous terrain, it would also be easy to guard against unwanted visitors.

In April 1943, the Manhattan Project was relocated to Los Alamos. It soon became a rambling small city of wooden barracks and other buildings. For the next two years, one of the most secret projects in the history of warfare would be undertaken there. Except for a few key government officials, no one, not even the wives of the participants, knew what was going on in that secluded location. Little did anyone realize that Los Alamos would be a name forever tied to the development of the most powerful weapon known to mankind.

In addition to the scientists, an army force was also stationed at Los Alamos. It had the job of administering the overall work of the project. It also provided the necessary security so that the scientists could work in complete secrecy. All mail and other communications were routed through Santa Fe, New Mexico. The political past and work history of each individual was closely investigated. Even the loyalty of Dr. Oppenheimer himself was questioned when it was discovered that he had some friends who had previously been involved with communism. However, these acquaintances proved not to be a problem, and he continued to direct the project brilliantly for its duration.

The huge uranium manufacturing facility at Oak Ridge, Tennessee, included not only dozens of factory buildings but also an entire city to house the workers and their families.

Production of Uranium and Plutonium

As part of the Manhattan Project, General Groves was responsible for the production of uranium and plutonium in sufficient quantity to meet the needs of the atomic scientists. The extensive research and testing by the scientists at Los Alamos determined that a uranium-powered bomb would need 220 pounds (100 kilograms) of U^{235} and a plutonium bomb would require only 4 1/2 pounds (2 kilograms) of that precious metal. Both of these rare metals were extremely difficult to produce and required the development of huge industrial plants to accomplish the task.

While the small band of dedicated scientists worked on their experiments at Los Alamos under the direction of Dr. Oppenheimer and his chief associates, Dr. Enrico Fermi and Dr. Edward Teller, vast numbers of individuals were involved in producing the rare metals needed. Two huge plants at Oak Ridge, Tennessee, with over 13,000 workers,

(Above) *FAT MAN. The huge 9,000 pound atomic bomb that was dropped on Nagasaki. This version was powered by the element plutonium.*

(Below) *LITTLE BOY. This uranium (U²³⁵) bomb was the one droped on Hiroshima by the Superfortress Enola Gay.*

were built to produce the U^{235} needed to create the first atomic bombs. A new city was built near the plants to house the army of workers and their families.

At the same time, another huge plant was built at Hanford, Washington, to produce plutonium. Some 50,000 men spent over a year building this huge facility. There they operated a nuclear reactor similar to the kind used to generate electricity today. The Hanford plant, utilizing uranium, created a controlled chain reaction that produced, as a by-product, the limited amount of plutonium needed for a second type of atomic bomb.

It is estimated that the Manhattan Project cost over two billion dollars before the first bomb was ready for testing.

Trinity—the Final Test

Through the more than two years from April 1943 to June 1945, General Grove's and Dr. Oppenheimer's teams of engineers and scientists had solved the problems of designing and creating an atomic bomb. As a matter of fact, they had actually designed three different types of bombs. The first, known as "Little Boy," received its tremendous explosive power from U^{235}. The second, a plutonium bomb, was called "Fat Man" because of its large round shape. These two bombs were soon to be used against Japan. A third type of bomb, deriving its power from hydrogen, would not be completed until 1952.

At the same time that the plans for an atomic bomb had been completed, the United States and its allies were preparing to invade Japan. President Harry S. Truman, who had become president earlier that year following the death of Franklin D. Roosevelt, was informed by the military that the invasion could result in as many as 500,000 American casualties. Because the Japanese leaders had indicated they would never surrender, the Japanese people would inevitably suffer far greater casualties and continued destruction of their homeland. As a result, President Truman had to decide if the atomic bomb should be used to prevent the terrible loss of life that would result from an invasion.

But the bomb had not even been tested. Even so, all components were ready for several bombs. The scientists and their assistants assembled one "Fat Man" bomb for a test. Final plans to stage "Trinity," the first test of a completed bomb, were underway at Los Alamos.

A remote air force bombing range at Alamogordo, New Mexico, was chosen as the site. A high metal tower was erected, and a "Fat Man" bomb was hoisted to its top. Finally, all preparations were completed for the first actual test of the world's most terrible weapon. The scientists and workers at the site withdrew to a concrete blockhouse five miles from the tower. On July 16, 1945, as the sun rose in the east, a huge fireball that was ten times brighter than the sun was formed as the deadly bomb exploded. A giant mushroom cloud rose into the sky above the site. The test tower evaporated in the heat of the blast, and the earth was burned to a crisp for miles around.

The first atom bomb had been exploded with the power of 20,000 tons—40 million pounds—of TNT. The atomic age, in all its horror was born.

Located five miles from the actual site of the first atomic bomb test, these earth-covered blockhouses protected scientists as they witnessed the resulting blast.

Chapter 2

IWO JIMA AND OKINAWA

In January 1945, although the United States was definitely winning the war, the Japanese were still fighting with all their might. The Allies' war against Japan had been going on for three long years since the sneak attack on Pearl Harbor in Hawaii. And for every victory there were thousands of American casualties. Tens of thousands of brave American soldiers, sailors and marines had died or had been wounded in the air, at sea or on the bloody beaches of Pacific islands like the Solomons, Kwajalein and Tarawa and in the jungles of New Guinea and the Philippines.

The U.S. commanders knew that victory would not come until the Japanese homeland was invaded and the spirit of the Japanese people broken. To accompish these two objectives, the United States needed to capture two key islands and establish bases from which attacks could be launched against the main Japanese islands of Kyushu and Honshu.

In the fall of 1944, plans were laid to set the stage for attacks on the main islands of Japan. The U.S. Navy, under the command of Admiral Chester Nimitz, was ordered to provide support to an invasion force of some 80,000 U.S. Marines that was to land on tiny Iwo Jima in the Volcano Islands 650 miles from Japan. The marines were to defeat its 20,000 Japanese defenders and establish air bases from which U.S. fighter aircraft could escort B-29 Superfortresses that were bombing Japanese cities. The invasion of Iwo Jima would take place during February of 1945 under the command of Major General Holland "Howling Mad" Smith.

At the same time, plans were also being made to invade and occupy the key Japanese island of Okinawa in April 1945. This large island in the Ryukyu chain, 700 miles southwest of Japan proper, would serve as a staging area from which U.S. troops could be prepared for the actual invasion of Japan. Lieutenant General Simon Bolivar Buckner would lead a force of 150,000 U.S. Army troops onto Okinawa.

The Battle for Iwo Jima

The Japanese high command had a clear understanding of the value of Iwo Jima. They had appointed a skilled Japanese general, Tadamichi Kuribayashi, to command the 20,000-man force defending the island. Every man knew that if they failed in turning back an invasion, they would never see their homeland again. They were well armed and prepared to fight to the finish. Their goal was to destroy ten Americans for every Japanese life lost.

Their defenses were so effective that even after 72 days of bombardment, the Japanese were still able to fight the invading U.S. Marines. However, after 36 days of fierce combat the battle for Iwo Jima was over. Almost 20,000 Japanese defenders died during the battle and only 216 were taken prisoner. The cost to the marines was also high. Some 6,800 were killed and over 20,000 were wounded. It was the most costly island invasion of the war to date.

However, the U.S. Marines had achieved the desired goals. The Iwo Jima airfields were quickly repaired. Even before the battle had ended, air force fighters were flying escort missions for the B-29s as they flew back and forth from Tinian and Saipan in the Marianas on bombing missions against Tokyo and other key Japanese targets.

Battle-damaged B-29s were able to land on the tiny island instead of being lost at sea. During the months that followed, some 2,400 B-29s used the Iwo Jima airfields for

U.S. troops climb up the rocky shore of Okinawa as they advance inland.

emergency landings. Many of their 27,000 crew members would have been lost if Iwo Jima had not been conquered. One author stated, "To the marines, Iwo looked like the ugliest place on earth, but B-29 pilots who made emergency landings months later called it the most beautiful. . . ."

Iwo Jima was a speck of land only eight square miles in area. It had taken ten weeks of aerial and naval bombardment and 36 days of hard-fought battles to defeat the enemy. If it took that long to conquer a tiny island at the cost of almost 30,000 casualties, what would it take to conquer the heavily defended Japanese homeland?

The Battle for Okinawa

A month after the fall of Iwo Jima, the U.S. forces embarked on what was to be the costliest campaign of the Pacific war. On April 1, 1945, an invasion force of some 170,000 U.S. soldiers and marines stormed ashore on the west coast of Okinawa. Supported by the U.S. Fifth Fleet and with complete air superiority, the landings proceeded smoothly. The U.S. forces quickly occupied the northern two-thirds of the island.

The initial targets, the Japanese airfields at Yontan and Kadena, were quickly captured. There was little, if any, opposition from the scattered Japanese troops confronted by the rapidly advancing Americans. Little did the Americans know that this was all part of the Japanese plan to defend the island.

Lieutenant General Mitsuru Ushijima, the Japanese commander, had ordered his troops to withdraw to the southern tip of the island, establishing hidden defense lines. The Japanese high command was planning to unleash hundreds, even thousands, of *kamikaze* "divine wind" suicide aircraft against the invading fleet and their escorting warships. After the kamikazes had destroyed much of the U.S. fleet, the invading force would be without supplies and air support and would be easily destroyed by General Ushijima's well-trained Okinawa Home Guard and other elite Japanese troops.

Neither side realized at the outset that the battle for Okinawa would last more than three months. Both sides would suffer terrible casualties of men, planes and ships. Finally, the vastly superior U.S. Navy and its air force beat back wave after wave of kamikaze attacks. The planned Japanese victory at sea and in the air did not happen. The battle for Okinawa soon became a deadly day-by-day and yard-by-yard battle for the Japanese stronghold surrounding the ancient town of Shuri in southern Okinawa.

"Blowtorch and Corkscrew"

As the U.S. Army and U.S. Marines battled southward, they were confronted by thousands of Japanese hidden in caves and tunnels on steep hillsides. Under heavy rains, the Americans struggled through mud and jungle to dig out the dry, well-armed and well-positioned Japanese. By sheer force of numbers they succeeded. They used what was called the "blowtorch and corkscrew" technique. As a Japanese cave position was discovered, it would be blasted with flamethrowers and then sealed shut with hand grenades and explosives.

*Victorious U.S. troops on Okinawa step around a dead Japanese soldier
as the last land battle of the war draws to a close.*

The battle for Okinawa continued in this fashion for
months. It had taken from April 1, 1945, until the middle of
June before an American victory was in sight. But at great
cost. On June 18, the American commander, Lieutenant
General Buckner, was killed by Japanese artillery fire. By
June 22, when Okinawa had officially fallen, some 130,000
Japanese had died and thousands had been taken prisoner.
The American casualties on land numbered in excess of
60,000, with some 16,000 killed.

Reviewing the outcome of this fiercely contested and
costly action, American authorities estimated that an invasion of the main Japanese islands would result in American
casualties of at least 500,000. Would Japan surrender before
an invasion became necessary? Would the United States
seek a peaceful solution rather than risk half a million more
American lives?

The need to use the ultimate weapon—an atomic
bomb—became stronger with each passing day.

Chapter 3

Firebombing Japan

The successes of the U.S. Army, Marines and Army Air Force (USAAF) along with the victorious campaigns waged by U.S. Navy warships, submarines and aircraft now gave the United States and its allies control of the entire Pacific region except for the main islands of Japan itself. The major targets of Iwo Jima and Okinawa had fallen. The next target was the enemy's homeland.

The USAAF, under the command of General Henry H. (Hap) Arnold, thought they could bomb the Japanese into submission. Still others in the army and navy felt that an invasion of Japan was the only answer to final victory. As 1944 drew to a close, final plans were being drawn for both courses of action.

B-29 Superfortresses

The USAAF had built its plan for victory around the huge new B-29 bomber. This giant bomber, using all of the latest developments of aeronautical science, could fly a distance of 3,500 miles and could carry a bombload of 8,000 pounds. In early 1944, the 20th Bomber Command was set up in India. Flying from bases in India and western China, it carried out attacks on Japanese bases in southeast Asia, in China and on southern Japanese islands. At first the B-29s had little success and suffered heavy losses due to me-

A fire storm sweeps through a Japanese city following firebombing by U.S. Air Force bombers.

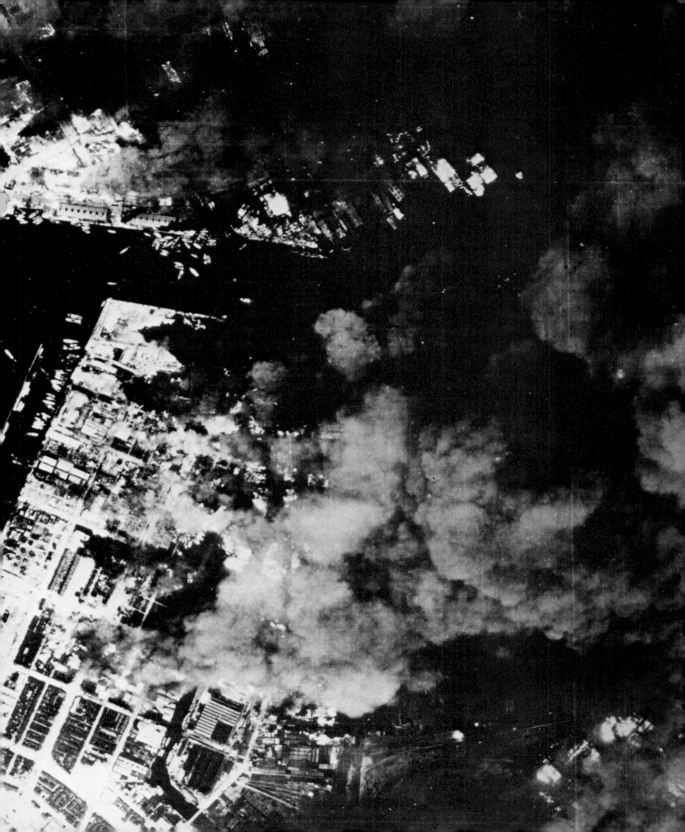

chanical failure, bad weather and enemy action. These problems were soon overcome, however, and each raid became more successful.

Later that year, the 21st Bomber Command was established in the Pacific after the capture of the islands of Tarawa, Guam and Tinian in the Marianas. These islands provided airfields close enough to Japan so that the B-29s could carry out long-range missions against cities on the main Japanese islands for the first time. On November 24, 1944, the first major B-29 attack was carried out against Tokyo.

In January 1945, Major General Curtis LeMay was put in command of the 21st Bomber Command in the Marianas. He used his skills learned as a commander of B-17s in Europe. He continued with ongoing long-range attacks on Japanese targets. High-level precision bombing missions were utilized but still with limited success. The bombers had to fly too high for accurate bombing. If they flew lower, they were under attack by Japanese fighters including kamikaze-style ramming attacks. The resulting heavy B-29 losses brought about the need for the campaign to capture Iwo Jima.

Low-Level Nighttime Attacks

The Japanese high command and the Japanese people were confident that they could withstand the bombing attacks on their homeland. They set up elaborate air-raid defenses and thought they were prepared to deal with whatever attacks might come. However, General LeMay had experimented with low-level as well as high-level attacks. On two occasions, large numbers of B-29s carrying incendiary bombs met with great success as resulting fires destroyed a large portion of their targets.

Finally, in March 1945, General LeMay started the tactics that he and his Washington superiors thought would end the war. Tokyo, the capital of Japan, was hit with the first fire raid. Flying under cover of darkness at the low altitude of 5,000 feet, 325 B-29s dropped some 150,000 pounds (75 tons) of incendiary and high-explosive bombs on their target. The results were horrendous, and the bombers returned to their bases with a loss of only 14 aircraft.

Tokyo Fire Storm

Firebombing attacks continued against many other major Japanese cities. Missions of up to 500 B-29s were carried out regularly against as many as half a dozen cities a day. On the night of March 9, Tokyo itself became the target once again. Pathfinder planes led the way and dropped highly flammable napalm (jellied gasoline) bombs to mark the target areas. Before the night was over, some 2,000 tons of incendiary bombs had been dropped on the helpless city. With a strong wind blowing, fires spread rapidly. Air-raid precautions and firefighting efforts were meaningless. Within a short time the heat of the flames generated violent air currents that swept a fire storm across the city.

Over 50 percent of Tokyo was destroyed. Although it was impossible to count the dead, it is estimated that as many as 200,000 Japanese died that night. To all who viewed the devastation in the cities that had been subjected to firebombings, it appeared that Japan was crippled. Normal civilian life had been brought to an end. The Japanese navy no longer existed. Much of Japan's war industry had been heavily bombed and almost destroyed. The U.S. generals thought that Japan would certainly surrender.

Japan was completely incapable of carrying on extended full-scale war. However, its military leaders refused to surrender. Over two million men of the Imperial Japanese Army and some 10,000 aircraft—mostly kamikaze—were still available to fight an invasion. The Japanese generals insisted on fighting to the bitter end in the hope that they could achieve an honorable peace. Little did they know what would happen next.

Chapter 4

INVASION PLANS

Considering the heavy casualties inflicted on American troops on Iwo Jima and Okinawa, it would seem that plans for an invasion of Japan would be held back. In addition, General LeMay's B-29s were having great success in the bombing of Japanese cities so that the possibility of a Japanese surrender appeared more likely every day.

Also, the blockade of Japan by the U.S. Navy was achieving great success. From May 1942 until April 1945, the U.S. Navy had sunk four million tons of Japanese ships—over two-thirds of their merchant fleet and most of their navy. As a result, Japan's people and its war industry were deprived of much needed food, oil, munitions and other supplies. The nation was starving. However, the Japanese military leaders insisted that the nation continue to fight.

MacArthur Plans Invasion

After the death of General Buckner, General Joseph Stilwell was brought in to take command of the U.S. 10th Army on Okinawa. His job was to turn Okinawa into a major base to support further aerial bombardment of Japan and the planned invasion. The soldiers and marines who had fought on Okinawa and Iwo Jima certainly hoped that the war would end before they had to attack the fanatical Japanese on their home ground.

On May 25, General Douglas MacArthur, following his victories in the Philippines, had been made commander of all United States Army troops in the Pacific. He had also

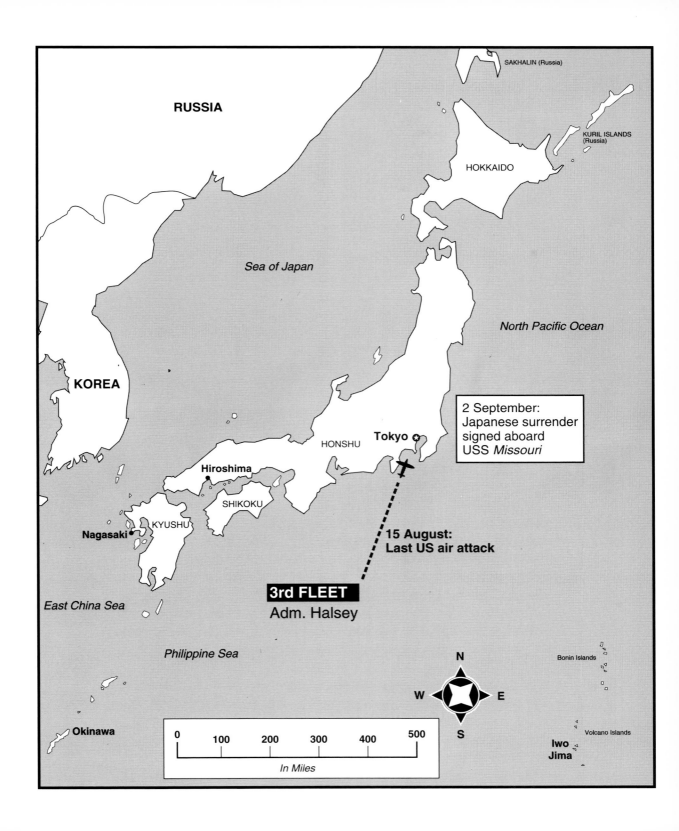

been appointed commander for the invasion of Japan, which had been named "Operation Downfall."

The U.S. Joint Chiefs of Staff were preparing for at least another full year of war. The invasion of the Japanese island of Kyushu (Operation Olympic) was scheduled for November 1, 1945, and the invasion of the main island of Honshu (Operation Coronet) was scheduled for March 1, 1946. The blockading of Japanese ports and the bombing of Japanese cities continued.

Japanese Prepare Defenses

Ketsu-Go was the Japanese name for its plan to defend its homeland. Even though the U.S. Navy and the USAAF were operating around and over Japan with little opposition, the Japanese still tried to fight back. Some 60 industrial cities had been heavily damaged by high-explosive and incendiary bombs. In July, still rejecting all Allied surrender demands, the Japanese military leaders began to put the *Ketsu-Go* plan into effect.

Two huge armies were formed around the Imperial Japanese Army of 2,300,000 troops. They were backed up by the militia, or national guard, of 28,000,000. The air force had hoarded some 10,000 aircraft of all types, and the navy had kept hundreds of small attack boats hidden from the enemy. Manned by special attack forces called *tokku*, these suicide craft and the kamikaze aircraft of the air force would attack the approaching invasion force far out to sea. Then, additional special attack forces would engage in further suicide attacks using various explosive-laden craft, human torpedoes, and other means of fighting the enemy as they approached the beaches.

Some Japanese Leaders Strive for Peace

While the military leaders found the idea of surrender completely impossible, many Japanese leaders felt otherwise. Commencing in January 1945, following the fall of

As the war drew to a close, the U.S. Navy defeated the Japanese navy and completely blockaded the islands of Japan.

Luzon in the Philippines, Emperor Hirohito had met with key civilian members of the government to find a way to end the war honorably. Right up to the end of the war, the military wanted to continue the fight while more level-headed leaders, knowing that the war was lost, wanted peace.

Although Russia had not yet declared war against Japan, it was carrying on discussions with Japanese leaders, trying to bring about peace. The Russians were taking this action in the hope of acquiring certain northern Japanese islands and Japanese-controlled Mongolia. The Japanese hoped that Russia would help them bring about peace on terms more favorable to the Japanese.

Meanwhile, at his headquarters in the Philippines, General MacArthur continued his plans for an invasion of the Japanese homeland. At home, at Los Alamos, General Groves and Dr. Oppenheimer proceeded with Trinity and the final successful testing of the first atomic bomb.

On July 27, 1945, following the Japanese official rejection of Allied surrender demands, President Truman ordered that two atomic bombs be prepared for use by August 3, 1945.

Chapter 5

THE ENOLA GAY

While at the Potsdam Conference in Germany (a meeting of the Allied leaders), President Truman received word that a bomb had been tested successfully. He immediately ordered that the necessary fissionable materials—U^{235} and plutonium and all the other necessary components to assemble several bombs—be delivered to the USAAF base on Tinian Island. However, he was still struggling with the final decision of whether or not to use the bomb. After careful consideration and much soul-searching, President Truman and his advisers agreed that the bomb should be used. This was undoubtedly one of the most difficult decisions faced by anyone in the history of mankind. The alternative was invasion of Japan, the possible loss of up to 500,000 Allied troops and the possible loss of a much larger number of Japanese soldiers and civilians.

Delivery and Assembly of the Bomb

The scientists at Los Alamos had perfected two types of bombs—"Little Boy," powered by uranium, and, "Fat Man," powered by plutonium. The components to assemble one of each type were sent to Tinian in July 1945. The navy cruiser USS *Indianapolis* delivered two unassembled bombs to Tinian on July 26. President Truman also issued orders that the bombs were to be ready to be dropped on August 3 unless the order was canceled by him.

Navy Captain William Parsons, a naval bomb expert who had been trained in the handling and construction of an atomic bomb, was in charge of the bombs on Tinian. He was responsible for their assembly. And, most difficult of

Navy Captain William Parsons (left) *and Colonel Paul W. Tibbets, Jr., brief the crew of the* Enola Gay *prior to the Hiroshima mission.*

all, he was to fly on the B-29 assigned to carry the bomb on the first mission. It was his decision to complete the final arming of the bomb after takeoff. He insisted on this procedure so that there would be no premature explosion of the bomb if the plane crashed during takeoff.

After working around the clock for almost a week, Captain Parsons completed the assembly of a "Little Boy" type bomb. Weighing 4 1/2 tons, it was ready to be hung in the center of the specially constructed bomb bay of a B-29. All was ready for the final order to deliver the world's first atomic bomb.

The Enola Gay and Its Crew

Not just any B-29 squadron or any B-29 crew would be given the vital task of delivering the bomb. A select group of B-29 crews was chosen and formed into the 509th Composite Group. They were not sent to the Pacific but were stationed at a secret base in Utah to receive special training. None knew what their final mission would be. All they knew was that they were being trained to drop heavy, odd-shaped bombs from high altitudes with pinpoint accuracy. They were also taught to leave the target area with steep, almost aerobatic diving turns immediately after dropping their bomb.

Once these crews arrived on Tinian, they were housed securely behind high fences. They flew no missions and were not allowed to mingle with other crew members on the base. Through the fences that separated them, they had to undergo the taunts and angry comments of the regular B-29 crews that had flown many missions and suffered heavy losses.

Finally, however, early on August 6 the crew that was to fly the first atomic bombing mission learned the nature of their mission. Colonel Paul Tibbets, Jr., the pilot, had been informed of the mission two days earlier. The commander of all USAAF units in the Pacific, General Carl "Tooey" Spaatz briefed Tibbets personally.

Their B-29 was the *Enola Gay*, named after Tibbets's mother. Tibbets's six crew members were then called together along with Captain Parsons. Captain Parsons described the bomb to them and showed pictures of the test that had taken place at Alamogordo, New Mexico. He described the bomb as the newest and most destructive bomb in the history of warfare. It was never described as being a nuclear weapon.

Two key members of the crew were Captain Theodore Van Kirk, the navigator, who had the critical task of delivering the plane over the target exactly on time and at the right altitude, and Major Tom Ferebee, an experienced bombardier. He could drop a bomb from 36,000 feet to a point within a circle only 300 feet in diameter.

Captain Parsons was the actual mission commander since he was responsible for arming the bomb and determining that everything was in order for the completion of the mission.

The Mission

Shortly after midnight on August 6, 1945, three B-29s took off from Tinian. They were weather ships that were to fly to three different targets in Japan. If weather was bad

The B-29 Superfortress, Enola Gay, *on the ground at its base in the Marianas*

over Hiroshima, the number one target, the *Enola Gay* could be directed to another target that was clear.

A short time later, Colonel Tibbets and his crew completed their preflight check of the aircraft, and Captain Parsons and his assistants made a final check of "Little Boy." All was ready. The engines were started, and the *Enola Gay* taxied to the end of the runway. Finally, at 2:45 A.M. Colonel Tibbets received a "clear for takeoff" message from the control tower, and the heavily laden plane started its roll down the runway to keep its date with destiny.

Colonel Tibbets pushed the great plane's four throttles to full power. Its huge 2,200-horsepower engines throbbed with explosive power as they pulled the B-29 down the runway. The pilot held the plane down to gain maximum speed before pulling back on the control column. As the plane reached the end of the 10,000-foot runway, it slowly lifted into the air and was on its way.

Shortly after takeoff, Captain Parsons and a helper crawled back into the bomb bay to start arming the bomb. Crowded by the 10-foot-long "Little Boy," the belly of the aircraft was poorly lit and noisy. But these factors did not bother Captain Parsons as he had practiced arming the bomb by activating its fuse both on the ground and in the aircraft dozens of times. Soon the bomb was ready.

As they reached their cruising altitude, Colonel Tibbets turned over the piloting of the aircraft to his copilot. One by one he visited with his fellow crew members to be certain all was going well and to answer any questions. The *Enola Gay* was accompanied by two other superfortresses that were to observe the entire mission and obtain a photographic record of the results. All three of the giant B-29s moved steadily through a cloudless sky toward Hiroshima.

Finally, at 7:24 A.M. the *Enola Gay* received a message from the weather aircraft that had preceded them. They were advised that the weather over Hiroshima was almost clear of cloud and they should continue with that ill-fated city as their primary target. On the ground, the Japanese had sighted that B-29 as it approached, and Hiroshima air-raid warnings sounded. However, since it did not appear to be a major raid, the warnings were canceled.

At 8:12 A.M., Captain Theo Van Kirk, the navigator, indicated that they were ready to start their bombing run. They were flying at 31,600 feet and were about 30 miles from their target. Colonel Tibbets turned control of the aircraft over to the bombardier, Major Tom Ferebee. He would guide the plane on automatic pilot on its final bomb run and release "Little Boy" at the proper moment. At that point, Colonel Tibbets ordered all crew members to put on special dark glasses that would protect their eyes from the bomb blast.

Slowly the seconds ticked by. At 8:15:17 Ferebee shouted, "Bombs away." Colonel Tibbets immediately took over the controls and threw the giant plane into a near vertical 150-degree diving turn to head away from the coming bomb blast.

The crews of the *Enola Gay* and their escorting B-29s waited breathlessly as "Little Boy" dropped steadily toward the unsuspecting city below.

Chapter 6

HIROSHIMA

At 8:16 A.M. on August 6, 1945, another normal business day was about to start in Hiroshima. Although one of Japan's largest industrial centers, the city had suffered little bomb damage up to this date. Air-raid warnings had been sounded earlier that day but had been canceled. The vapor trails seen high above the city were the only sign of enemy aircraft in the area. Suddenly, however, people near the center of the city heard the loud noise of a diving aircraft high above. Looking up, a few people saw a parachute pop open and drift downward carrying a heavy load. Then there was a blinding light, brighter than a thousand suns . . . and then there was death.

The *Enola Gay* had dropped its deadly cargo so that it exploded at 2,000 feet, directly above the central business district of Hiroshima. Its fuse had been set so the bomb would explode at that altitude to do the maximum amount of damage. The 4 1/2-ton bomb exploded with the force of 20,000 tons of TNT. Its fireball equaled the heat of the sun's surface, some 300,000 degrees centigrade. At ground zero, the point directly below the blast, the temperature was estimated at close to 6,000 degrees centigrade.

Heat, Blast and Radioactivity

Heat from the tremendous chain reaction that created the blast accounted for incredible damage. Stone buildings and paved streets bubbled and buckled. Humans, animals and all vegetation near the center were simply turned to vapor. All wooden structures within two miles of ground zero immediately burst into flame.

Heat, however, accounted for only a portion of the damage. Another third of the damage created by the bomb was the result of the blast. The compressed and heated air expanded at the rate of four tons per square yard and raced outward from the center at a speed of more than 1,000 feet per second. Only a few reinforced concrete buildings could withstand the tremendous forces of the blast.

Another third of the eventual damage to the people of Hiroshima was caused by radioactivity. After the horror of the destructive heat and explosion, huge amounts of deadly gamma rays had been released. In the days to come, thousands would die from radiation poisoning. Many more would suffer and die from the effects during the months and years that followed this holocaust.

The View from Above

At first, the crew of the *Enola Gay* could see or feel none of the effects of the exploding bomb. Their black glasses shielded them from the glare of the fireball. In the initial moments of their diving escape from the scene, they could neither feel nor hear what was happening on the ground six miles below. However, a few seconds later they were hit. The powerful shock wave and the sound from the blast had caught up with them. The huge plane was tossed about like a ship on a stormy sea. Colonel Tibbets thought they had been hit by anti-aircraft fire. Bringing his plane back under control, he heard the rumbling noise of the atom bomb blast and realized they had been caught in the wall of air blasted out from the center of the explosion.

One of the bomber's crew members gave a vivid eyewitness account over the *Enola Gay's* intercom system:

"A column of smoke rising fast. It has a fiery red core. A bubbling mass, purple gray in color, with that red core. It's all turbulent. Fires are springing up everywhere, like flames shooting out of a huge bed of coals . . . Here it comes, the

The crew members of the Enola Gay viewed this mushroom cloud from the air following their delivery of the first atomic bomb dropped on an enemy target.

mushroom shape . . . It's like a mass of bubbling molasses
. . . it's nearly level with me and climbing . . ."

A few hours later, the *Enola Gay* landed at Tinian—
mission accomplished. At 2:58 P.M. the huge bomber rolled
to a stop on the ramp at the airfield. The nature of the
mission and the successful result had been announced.
Bands were playing, and the whole base had turned out to
welcome back the victorious crew and their escorting B-29s.
General Spaatz and General LeMay greeted Colonel Tibbets
as he stepped from the aircraft. General Spaatz congratu-
lated him and his crew and pinned the Distinguished Service Cross on Colonel Tibbets's wrinkled flight suit.

Meanwhile, back at Los Alamos, the news had reached
the headquarters of the Manhattan Project. Captain Parsons
had radioed a message back to Dr. Oppenheimer immediately after the bomb had been dropped. "Little Boy" had
been delivered to Hiroshima successfully. Oppenheimer and
his staff were overjoyed. Their years of hard work had
finally paid off.

Death on Every Side

It is estimated that some 130,000 residents of Hiroshima
were killed that day or would eventually die from the effects of the bomb. Where it normally took thousands of
bombs to destroy a target, only one bomb had laid waste an
entire city of 350,000 people.

Most people near the center of the city died instantly.
There were some freak cases where people survived, protected by some of the heavily reinforced buildings. For
those who survived, the blast area became a living hell.
Tens of thousands were burned and bleeding from wounds
of every description. And there was no one to offer immediate help. Many were blinded by the glare of the fireball.

Commuter trains and vehicles on the streets had been
stopped or destroyed in their tracks. Their occupants had

All that is left of one Shinto shrine in Nagasaki. Because the blast could go through and around the structure it escaped damage while almost everything around it was destroyed.

been incinerated where they sat. Most survivors were in a complete state of shock regardless of their injuries. Many wandered around naked and covered with burns. Their clothes had literally been ripped from their bodies by the blast. For the first hours there was no help available from any source or direction.

Damage Reports Unbelievable

No one believed the first reports of the disaster that reached Tokyo. A reporter who had witnessed the explosion at some distance from the city thought an ammunition factory had exploded. He jumped into his car and raced toward Hiroshima. Only when he could witness the damage and death at first hand did he realize what had happened.

However, when he reported the extent of the damage to his newspaper in Tokyo, no one believed him. No bomb existed that could do such damage was the opinion expressed by those receiving the first reports.

Finally, when accurate reports did reach Tokyo, the Japanese cabinet met and then informed the Emperor. Prime Minister Suzuki advised the Emperor to accept the Allied demands and surrender immediately. However, the Supreme War Direction Council still would not consider surrender and insisted that the war go on. The militarists still felt they could fight off an invasion and would accept a peace only on their own terms.

Everything changed on August 9 when "Fat Man," the plutonium bomb, was dropped on Nagasaki. Some 25,000 more Japanese died that day. And to add insult to injury, the Russians, realizing that the war was about to end, declared war against Japan.

This burn victim, although severely burned by radiation, was partially protected by the pattern of her dress.

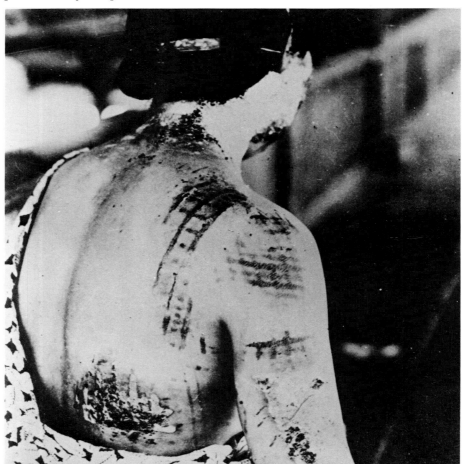

With the exception of a few reinforced concrete buildings the cities of Hiroshima and Nagasaki were flattened by the tremendous force of the atomic bombs.

When no immediate response was received from the Japanese, conventional bombing was resumed against Japan.

Prime Minister Churchill of Great Britain was to write after the war had ended:

"To avert a vast, indefinite butchery, to bring the war to an end, to give peace to the world, to lay healing hands upon a tortured peoples by a manifestation of overwhelming power at the cost of a few explosions, seemed, after all our toils and peril, a miracle of development.

"British consent in principle to the use of the weapon had been given on July 4th (1945), before the test had taken place. The final decision now lay in the main with President Truman, who had the weapon: but I never doubted since that he was right."

Chapter 7

JAPAN SURRENDERS

The possibility of surrender by Japan was a severe blow to the sense of honor of its people. Japan was a country that had never lost a war. They worshiped their emperor as a god. They feared the complete destruction of their society and their way of life if they were forced into an unconditional surrender to the Allies.

Faced with defeat after defeat, many of Japan's leaders knew that the war was lost. However, complete surrender could not be considered. Moderates in the government favored seeking peace while the military leaders favored fighting on to the bitter end. Emperor Hirohito was helpless to direct Japan's future course as his ministers fought among themselves.

The First Talks of Peace

Prime Minister Hideki Tojo had headed the Japanese government from 1941 until mid-1944. He also served as War Minister and Army Chief of Staff during that period. However, after the Japanese defeat in the Marianas, he was forced out of office. Peace advocates formed a new government. They began efforts to have the war ended by imperial decree from Emperor Hirohito and to save face by blaming Tojo and the military. However, military and civilian leaders rejected the idea as they believed the Allies would demand an unconditional surrender.

The next efforts came in January 1945 as General MacArthur was recapturing the Philippines. Emperor

B-29 Superfortresses continued conventional bombing of Japan when Japan refused to surrender even after the atomic bombs were dropped.

Hirohito called together the *jushin* (former prime ministers and other government leaders) to discuss peace. These discussions produced no meaningful results as the military members of the government insisted on continuing to fight.

The Supreme War Direction Council

In April 1945, following the fall of Iwo Jima and the invasion of Okinawa, the peace-seeking members of the government forced the appointment of Admiral Baron Kantaro Suzuki as prime minister. Although a retired naval officer, he was a moderate with no known connection to the militarists. An all-new Supreme War Direction Council was formed with Admiral Suzuki at its head, but it was made up of three moderates who favored peace and three militarists who favored carrying on the war. The army forced the new council and the government to agree to fight to the finish, to combine the army and the navy and to take the necessary measures to insure victory in the invasion of Japan that was sure to come. The military leaders were filled with the age-old spirit of the *samurai* (the military leaders of ancient Japan). The idea of surrender was unthinkable.

No Way to Wage All-out War

In spite of the great demands made by the militarists, Japan was in no condition to continue the war. The entire nation was on the verge of starvation, all military ammunition and equipment were in short supply and many of the soldiers and airmen who remained were untrained. Even the Imperial Japanese Army was comprised of many poor physical specimens who could not hold the respect of their officers or the Japanese people.

Emperor Hirohito was convinced by his advisers that the war must be ended. To accomplish this goal, he sent representatives to Moscow to ask the Russians to help bring about an honorable peace between the Allies and Japan. Russia had not declared war on Japan at that time. However, as long as the Allies insisted on unconditional surrender, there was no basis for discussion as the Japanese military would not consider such an end to the war.

The Japanese surrender team on the USS Missouri *prior to the signing of the surrender documents*

Surrounded by officers of the United States and the Allies, General Douglas MacArthur, the Allied Supreme Commander in the Pacific, signs the surrender documents officially ending the war with Japan.

The Potsdam Declaration

An historic meeting between the United States, Great Britain, China and Russia was held at Potsdam, Germany, from July 17 to August 2, 1945. At this meeting the leaders discussed the continuation of the war, the possible surrender of Japan and post-war relationships between the combatants and their allies. Of particular importance at that meeting was a message from the United States, Great Britain and China to Japan demanding an immediate unconditional surrender. This was sent at a time when only President Truman, Great Britain's prime minister, Winston Churchill, and their top advisers were aware of the existence of an atomic weapon.

The Potsdam Declaration, demanding the surrender of Japan, was delivered on July 26, 1945. With completely mixed emotions, the Japanese Supreme War Direction Council took no immediate action. In fact, Prime Minister Suzuki said he would reject the proposal "with silence." Finally, however, on July 28, the prime minister did publicly announce the rejection of the demand and stated that Japan would ". . . resolutely fight for the successful conclusion of this war."

Hiroshima and Nagasaki, the Final Blow

Following the news of the dropping of the bomb on Hiroshima on August 6 and its terrible results, the Emperor was advised to accept the surrender demands. However, the Supreme War Direction Council took no action. As a result of their lack of activity, President Truman ordered the dropping of the second bomb on Nagasaki on August 9. This, along with the declaration of war on Japan by the Russians, finally moved the Supreme War Direction Council to consider surrender.

The big concern was what would happen to the Emperor and the Imperial Japanese Government after surrender. Would there be a complete loss of face, and would the emperor be treated as another war figure or even as a war criminal? With the council still deadlocked, they finally asked the emperor for his opinion. Although the emperor had been in favor of ending the war for some time he had been overruled by the miltary members of the council. At last, to his great credit and regardless of the consequences, he immediately stated that he wanted peace.

On August 10, the Japanese Foreign Office notified the Allies that they accepted the Potsdam Declaration ". . . with the understanding that the said declaration does not compromise any demand which prejudices the prerogatives of His Majesty as Sovereign Ruler."

Because of the uncertainty of this answer, the Allies

Supreme Allied Commander General Douglas MacArthur and Emperor Hirohito are shown here after the surrender of Japan.

Swarms of U.S. military aircraft fly in formation over the U.S. fleet during surrender ceremonies that were taking place aboard the USS Missouri.

continued their bombing of Japanese targets but without the use of atomic bombs. Finally, Emperor Hirohito urged the government to accept the terms of surrender including the fact that he personally would be subject to the direction of the Supreme Commander of the Allied Powers. This courageous action was almost stopped when a group of fanatical Japanese officers tried to take over the Imperial Palace and the emperor and cancel the plans for surrender. This action was stopped, and on August 15, 1945, a radio message from the emperor to the Japanese people was aired announcing the surrender.

Loyalty to the emperor prevailed, and the surrender proceeded in an orderly fashion. On September 2, 1945, the formal surrender documents were signed as members of the nations involved met on the battleship USS *Missouri*. General Douglas MacArthur, as Allied Supreme Commander, and representatives of the United States, Great Britain and Australia signed for the Allies. Japanese Foreign Minister Mamoru Shigemitsu signed for the Japanese.

World War II was over!

Crowds of Americans celebrated in the streets in American cities from coast to coast following the announcement of Japan's unconditional surrender to the Allies on August 14, 1945.

GLOSSARY

Allies The nations that joined together during World War II to defeat Germany and Japan: Great Britain, the United States, China, the Soviet Union and France.

atom The smallest particle of an element that can exist either alone or in combination.

atomic bomb A bomb that derives its power from the release of atomic energy.

atomic energy The energy released from the splitting of an atomic nucleus.

automatic pilot A system of controls on an airplane that keeps it in straight and level flight without the assistance of a human pilot.

battleship The largest modern warship.

chain reaction The activity that occurs within an atomic bomb. A sustaining nuclear reaction is one in which each reaction exceeds the one preceding it, thus releasing tremendous amounts of explosive energy.

cruiser A high-speed warship, next in size to a battleship.

fire storm Fires which spread rapidly due to the high winds generated by the heat of the fires caused by incendiary bombs.

gamma rays Electromagnetic radiation released by the explosion of an atomic bomb.

kamikaze Means "divine wind" in Japanese. The name given to pilots, aircraft or attacks involving suicide missions against Allied ships during World War II.

neutron A subatomic particle found within the nucleus of an atom.

nuclear Pertains to the central nucleus of an atom of an element. It is also the type of warfare involving atomic or hydrogen bombs.

nuclear reactor A device in which a nuclear chain reaction is created and controlled.

radiation The combined processes of emission, transmission and absorption of radiant energy.

samurai Means "warrior" in Japanese. Refers to the military traditions found in ancient Japanese history.

TNT A widely used explosive, trinitrotoluene.

unconditional surrender The absolute surrender of a military force or a country at war without conditions or limitations.

INDEX

Alamogordo, New Mexico 12, 28
Arnold, General Henry H. 18
Asia 18
atomic bomb 6, 7, 11, 12, 17, 25,
    32, 33, 37, 39
atomic scientists 9
Australia 44
Austria 5

B-17 Flying Fortress 20
B-29 Superfortress 13, 14, 15, 18,
    20, 21, 22, 27, 28, 29, 30, 34,
    39
Blowtorch and Corkscrew 16
Buckner, Lieutenant General
    Simon Bolivar 14, 17, 22

China 18, 41
Churchill, Prime Minister Winston
    37, 41
Columbia University, NY 6

Distinguished Service Cross 34

Einstein, Albert 7
Enola Gay 26, 27, 28, 29, 30, 31,
    32, 33, 34
Europe 20

Fat Man 11, 12, 36
Ferebee, Major Tom 28, 30
Fermi, Dr. Enrico 3, 7, 9
Firebombing 21
509th Composite Group 27
Frisch, Otto Robert 5

gamma rays 32
Germany 6, 26
Great Britain 5, 37, 41, 44

Groves, Brigadier General
    Leslie R. 7, 8, 9, 11, 25
Guam Island 20

Hanford, Washington 11
Hirohito, Emperor 25, 36, 38, 40,
    42, 43, 44
Hiroshima, Japan 27, 29, 30, 31,
    32, 34, 35, 37, 42
Hitler, Adolf 5
Honshu Island 13, 24

Imperial Japanese Army 21, 40
India 18
Indianapolis 26
Iwo Jima 13, 14, 18, 22, 39

Japan 7, 11, 14, 18, 22, 24, 26, 28,
    38, 42
jushin 38

Kadena, Japan 15
kamikaze (divine wind) aircraft
    16, 20, 21, 24
Ketsu-Go 24
Kuribayashi, General Tadamichi
    14
Kwajalein Islands 13
Kyushu Island 13, 24

LeMay, Major General Curtis 18,
    20, 22, 34
Little Boy 11, 26, 27, 29, 30, 34
Los Alamos, New Mexico 8, 9, 12,
    25, 26, 34
Luzon, Philippines 25

MacArthur, General Douglas 22,
    25, 38, 41, 43, 44

Manhattan Project 7, 8, 9, 11, 34
Marianas Islands 14, 20, 29, 38
Meitner, Lise 5
Missouri 40, 44
Mongolia 25
Moscow, Russia 40

Nagasaki, Japan 36, 37, 42
Netherlands 5
New Guinea 13
New York City, NY 7
Nimitz, Admiral Chester 13
Nuclear physicists 7

Oak Ridge, Tennessee 9
Okinawa 13, 14, 15, 16, 17, 18, 22,
    39
Operation Coronet 24
Operation Downfall 24
Operation Olympic 24
Oppenheimer, Dr. Julius Robert
    7, 8, 11, 25, 34

Parsons, Captain William 26, 27,
    28, 29, 30, 34
Pearl Harbor, Hawaii 7, 13
Philippines 13, 22, 25, 38
plutonium 6, 9, 11, 26, 36
Potsdam Conference 26
Potsdam Declaration 42
Potsdam, Germany 41

radiation poisoning 32
Roosevelt, President Franklin D.
    7, 11
Russia 25, 36, 41, 42
Ryukyu 14

Saipan Island 14
samurai 39

Santa Fe, New Mexico 8
Shigemitsu, Foreign Minister
    Mamoru 44
Shinto shrine 35
Shuri, Okinawa 16
Smith, Major General Holland 14
Solomon Islands 13
Spaatz, General Carl 28, 34
Stilwell, General Joseph 22
Suzuki, Admiral Baron Kantaro
    (Prime Minister) 36, 39, 42

Tarawa Island 13, 20
Teller, Dr. Edward 9
Tibbets, Colonel Paul W. Jr., 27,
    28, 29, 30, 32, 34
Tinian Island 14, 20, 26, 28, 34
Tojo, Prime Minister Hideki 38
tokku (suicide craft) 24
Tokyo, Japan 14, 20, 21, 35, 36
Trinity 12, 25
Truman, President Harry S. 11,
    12, 25, 26, 37, 41, 42

United States 5, 6, 13, 14, 15, 16,
    18, 22, 24, 41, 44
University of California, Berkley 7
University of Chicago 7
Uranium 235 (U^{235}) 5, 6, 9, 11, 26
USAAF (United States Army Air
    Force) 18, 24, 26
Ushijima, Lieutenant General
    Mitsuru 16
Utah 27

Van Kirk, Captain Theodore 28,
    30
Volcano Islands 13

Yontan, Japan 15